1950s AMERICAN FASHION

Jonathan Walford

CAPTIVATING . . . and it's Disciplined, too   Dress about $25

SH   NS

Published in Great Britain in 2012 by Shire Publications Ltd, Midland House, West Way, Botley, Oxford OX2 0PH, United Kingdom.

44-02 23rd Street, Suite 219, Long Island City, NY 11101, USA.

E-mail: shire@shirebooks.co.uk   www.shirebooks.co.uk

A CIP catalogue record for this book is available from the British Library.

Shire Library no. 695.   ISBN-13: 978 0 74781 164 0

Jonathan Walford has asserted his right under the Copyright, Designs and Patents Act, 1988, to be identified as the author of this book.

Designed by Tony Truscott Designs, Sussex, UK and typeset in Perpetua and Gill Sans.

Printed in China through Worldprint Ltd.

12 13 14 15 16   10 9 8 7 6 5 4 3 2 1

COVER IMAGE
See page 48.

TITLE PAGE IMAGE
Advertisement for Anne Fogarty, *Vogue* magazine, May 15, 1956.

CONTENTS PAGE IMAGE
Advertisement for Gay Gibson, a line of clothes made by the Gernes Garment Company, from *Vogue* magazine, January 1, 1957.

ACKNOWLEDGEMENTS
I am particularly grateful for the generous research provided by Lynne Kranieri, Bret Fowler, and Christ Stoeckel; for the helpful assistance provided by many members of the Vintage Fashion Guild, especially Elizabeth Bramlett, as well as the invaluable help of Kenn Norman in pulling everything together; and for Kelli Christiansen for her editorial expertise.

All photos are by the author and are of garments in the Fashion History Museum in Cambridge, Ontario, but for the Grenelle-Estévez sack dress illustrated on page 12, the Ceil Chapman cocktail dress illustrated on page 19, and the Herbert Sondheim cocktail dress illustrated on page 24, which are from the Seneca Fashion Resource Centre in Toronto, Ontario; the Grenelle-Estévez dress illustrated on page 29 is from the private collection of Joseph Hisey, Stratford, Ontario; the Platter Pals felt skirt illustrated on page 39 and the leopard appliqué felt skirt illustrated on page 51 are from the private collection of Susan Langley, Rochester, New York.

Shire Publications is supporting the Woodland Trust, the UK's leading woodland conservation charity, by funding the dedication of trees.

CONTENTS

ORIGINS OF THE AMERICAN FASHION INDUSTRY

THE 1950s BELONGED TO AMERICA. The country led in postwar economic recovery and industrial production; refrigerators, televisions, and automobiles were churned out in huge quantities for the vast numbers of new families relocating to the sprawling suburbs. Despite a swing toward social and political conservatism in the 1950s, American culture was at the forefront of modern art—in painting, sculpture, theater, and literature, as well as contemporary music in the form of jazz and rock 'n' roll. In the field of design, American architects, furniture designers, and textile artists were internationally influential. And now even American fashion designers were being recognized as originators and leaders in their field.

The American fashion industry originated when the country became a leading industrialized nation in the late nineteenth century. The building of factories turned large towns into small cities and small cities into metropolises. Railroads crisscrossed the country, bringing goods manufactured east of the Mississippi River to the western frontier. What could not be found at local dry goods stores in the most rural locations could be ordered by mail from Chicago or New York, where, by the turn of the century, full-service department stores carried more ready-made fashions than ever before: corsets, shoes, petticoats, capes, stockings, hats, gloves, and wrappers (house dresses).

In the early twentieth century, American designers, both native born and naturalized, were hired by manufacturers to adapt Paris and London fashions for the American market. America was not yet confident in its ability to originate design, but it was confident in its ability to adapt fashion for mass production. New York became the center of the high-end ready-made trade, and by 1920, even the elite were buying New York ready-made clothes for everyday wear.

By the 1930s, America's international reputation as a creator of fashion was evident in Hollywood films, but while movie costumers received screen credits for their designs, most fashion designers still worked anonymously under manufacturer's labels, unless the designer was also the owner of the company. American fashion magazines continued to report on styles from Paris rather than about anything made by domestic design talent. This began to change when Stanley Marcus of the Dallas-based Neiman Marcus department store created an annual award for distinguished service in the field of fashion. The first awards, in 1938, were given to American and European designers, equating the two as equally important for the American market. Similarly, the Coty perfume company created an award in 1942 intended to promote American, especially New York, fashion and design.

After Paris was occupied by the Nazis in June 1940, American fashion journalists turned to American designers for fashion news to fill their magazines. When the United States also became involved in World War II after Pearl Harbor, the American fashion industry was hobbled by austerity measures that limited the type and amount of materials allowed for clothing production. Despite these restrictions, American fashion design flourished under the challenge to find clever and artistic ways to manipulate rationed materials. More designers opened for business during the war than ever before, and American women soon began recognizing the names of home-grown design talent.

Before World War II ended in the Pacific, Paris was already promoting its fashions in an attempt to regain its role as international style delineator. Within two years, Christian Dior launched a debut collection, in February 1947, which became the epitome of Paris's postwar regeneration. American fashion editor Carmel Snow of *Harper's Bazaar* was particularly enamoured with Dior, exclaiming his collection had a "New Look." However, the full-skirted, nipped-waist, soft-shouldered styles of Dior's collection were not universal hits with American women who did not want to be weighed down in corsets and crinolines like their grandmothers.

By 1951, it looked like Paris might be in charge again of high fashion silhouettes, but from New York's Seventh Avenue to California, American fashion was becoming increasingly self-determined, and by the end of the decade, the United States would be exporting styles back across the Atlantic to its former fashion mentors.

Sportswear separates were the strength of the American fashion industry. Haymaker Shirts, *Vogue* magazine, August 1, 1953.

all is fair in this tug of war! Even when yanked, crushed or twisted, Unidure-processed fabrics spring back into shape simply by hanging...without the chore of pressing. Wrinkle resistant not for just a day, not for just a year, but *always*–Unidure-processing is *guaranteed* for the life of the garment. The smartest rayon fashion fabrics this season–flannels, tweedy types, gabardines–boast of this special feature. So...for that trim 'n tidy look, with the minimum of effort ...buy spun rayon fashions and fabrics bearing the famous Unidure tag.

SEEING IS BELIEVING!

if it's tagged

UNIDURE®

It's permanently wrinkle resistant for the life of the garment

No pressing problems!
UNIDURE®
processed for permanent
WRINKLE-RESISTANCE

Capezio Sandals

THE AMERICAN LOOK—
HIGH FASHION

T HE ECONOMY OF THE EARLY 1950s was strong in the United States, but prices were on the rise, especially for clothing, and American women purchased their wardrobes carefully. Versatility became one way to counteract higher prices: reversible coats with sleeves that could be turned back into deep cuffs for a dressier "late day" look, décolleté dresses for dinner or theater that could be transformed into daytime outfits with the addition of a matching jacket, and suits with two skirts (pleated and straight) were all economical ways to stretch the clothing budget.

In 1950, daytime coats were full and flaring from the shoulders, but by fall 1951, narrow, column-shaped coats had debuted. Both styles were available simultaneously in many materials, especially in a newly imported French looped pile called "poodle" cloth that was quickly imitated by American textile manufacturers. By 1952, Parisian-designed full-skirted princess-line coats were being avidly copied by American designers. In fur, dark mink and sable were the most desirable—and least affordable—of all fur coats. Blonde furs, ranging from natural Aleutian mink at the high end to midpriced golden fox, down to bleached and dyed raccoon, gained popularity early in the decade. For those who could not afford a full coat or jacket, there were capes and stoles, especially of mink, fox, black seal, and rabbit.

The high cost of fur led to more interest in faux fur; nylon pile mouton "Teddy Bear" coats and jackets became a hit in 1952. The 1950s was the first decade to flaunt fakes of many types. If a woman could not afford a cashmere sweater, for example, an Orlon sweater looked almost as good. If she couldn't afford a sparkling diamond brooch, a "frankly fake" rhinestone floral or starburst spray worked just as well. Oversized rhinestone brooches were essential pieces of jewelry in the early 1950s. They appeared as often on tweed suits as on silk dresses. For evening, rhinestone necklace and earring sets were favorites, while multiple-strand fake pearl beads were popular for filling in suit necklines during the day.

Faux was everywhere, and synthetics became more popular as well. Many synthetic materials, some in development for more than a decade,

The thread of the story is LUREX

Lurex...black as shining jet, woven in silk by Rémond-Holland
...in a gown designed by Jean Dessès for Nanty Frocks.
At Gunther Jaeckel, New York: Neiman-Marcus, Dallas.
Lurex, non-tarnishing metallic yarn, made only by
The Dobeckmun Company, Cleveland 1, Ohio...New York: 250 West 57 Street.

Advertisement for Lurex thread, a brand name for a metallic filament fiber, from *Harper's Bazaar*, October 1952.

were commercially launched in the early 1950s, including Lurex, Pellon, Dacron, Dynel, Acrilan, Terylene, Arnel, Vicara, and Borgana. These new materials were usually washable and wrinkle free, and, when blended with a natural fiber, created a textile that often brought out the best qualities of both fibers. Orlon, introduced in 1952, was a huge success for sweaters. When blended with wool, the material was called "Lorette" and used for making permanent-pleat skirts.

The popularity of the new miracle fibers worried producers of traditional materials that they might be left out of the future. In April 1953, the U.S. secretary of agriculture, cognizant of the importance of cotton to the American economy, presented the first Cotton Fashion Award to American designer Adele Simpson.

But the future kept coming. New methods of production led to improvements in established materials, such as nylon. In 1950, the permanent-pleat heat process of nylon tricot was first used for making trims for nightgowns and slips. In 1951, "Petticoat fever" took over in fashion lingerie when three or more crinolines of nylon tricot, net, and taffeta were worn to give swirl and rustle to full-cut skirts. That same year, American manufacturers began using Pellon, a nonwoven textile, as an inexpensive stiffener to create full-skirted silhouettes.

Also in 1951, fourteen inches from the floor was recommended as the ideal daytime hemline. That same length was used for the short formal or "prom" dress, a debut style that combined the tulle and lace typical of an evening gown but in a daytime length. The following year, short formals adopted "ballerina-" or "waltz"-length hems, which were four inches longer than daytime hemlines.

Slim and full skirts coexisted in the early 1950s; narrower styles were generally better suited for daytime tailoring, while full skirts were preferred for late-day and formal occasions, although summery dresses often used full-skirt silhouettes. By 1952, suit jackets were being made shorter, ending at the top of the hip. With nipped waists, these feminine-shaped jackets were paired with fuller skirts for dressy suits, reviving Christian Dior's overtly feminine silhouette of spring 1947.

Dior had been dominating Paris fashion news for years, but his reign was about to be challenged by Balenciaga, whose designs were more architectural. In 1953, Balenciaga's suits featured stand-away collars and longer, unfitted jackets; the American copies were called "matchbox" suits. That year also saw the height of ensembles (dresses with matching coats or jackets). For fall, the contoured princess-line sheath made fashion news, again with a jacket or coat to make an ensemble.

After a fifteen-year absence due in part to World War II, Coco Chanel surprised the fashion world in spring 1954 by relaunching her Paris label with a small collection that was somewhat reminiscent of her 1920s work. Most fashion editors agreed it was a failure, and Chanel might have faded back into obscurity if it were not for American designers picking up on the easy elegance of the 1920s-influenced clothes. Most autumn 1954 collections in New York showed some influences, even though Chanel herself presented no collection that season. Straighter skirts, boxier jackets, shapeless coats, and a marked increase in costume jewelery permeated the shows.

Alongside dresses inspired by Chanel, fitted princess-line dresses were very popular. Full skirts were combined with the princess line by dropping the waist seam to the hip, highlighting the molded form of the torso. This was a popular look for late day and evening for the next two years, until 1956. Daytime dresses remained slim and

Brown and black wool tweed "Matchbox" suit, by Christian Dior New York, c. 1953–54.

Advertisement for Cotillion, from *Vogue* magazine, August 1, 1953, showing full- and waltz- (prom-) length evening gowns.

COTILLION makes you a picture to remember

34 (left). Floor-length drift of Beckendorf's billowing nylon net, lighted with lace. Beautiful beyond belief, that bare boned bodice. Red, blue, white. Sizes 7 to 15. $55.
35 (right). Unexpected, unforgettable, the short lace formal that uses a froth of Beckendorf's nylon net to define the drama of asymmetrical lines. Red, blue, white. Sizes 7 to 15. $55.

Pink silk chiffon evening gown with "intermission" hemline, by Don Loper couture, dated May 1954.

fitted, with short or no sleeves to feature a collection of jangling bracelets. For women who wanted a more demure look, there were jumper and middy styles, originally intended as junior fashions but now being made in sophisticated fabrics to appeal to a wider age range of women.

The well-established full-skirt silhouette remained popular for evening wear, but taffeta and satin pushed out the tulle concoctions of previous years. In 1954, bouffant ball gowns first appeared with "intermission" hemlines—a term coined by Pauline Trigere to refer to an above-ankle-length skirt in front, dipping to the ground at back. Instead of being strapless, most evening gowns were now cut with deep V necklines.

In 1955, long, slim evening gowns gained popularity. Dresses made from Indian saris, and similarly draped, were especially favored for being worn with summer tans. Fur gained importance for trimming wardrobes after 1955. Mink, leopard, and other short furs appeared as collars on tailored suits and evening jackets, while long-haired fox, lynx, and raccoon were used for glamor collars on tweed day clothes and town coats.

Cecil Beaton's 1912-inspired costumes for the Broadway hit *My Fair Lady* made a huge impact upon Seventh Avenue in 1956. The black-and-white Ascot scene (retained in the 1961 film) was particularly influential, with high-waisted Edwardian styles, almost universally in black, appearing in many collections for fall. A craze for historical styles also developed in jewelry; pieces were supposed to look inherited rather than recently purchased. Antique gold-finish lockets and cameo brooches picked up on the Edwardian craze. Almost every woman bought something inspired by *My Fair Lady*— a big hat, Louis-heeled pumps, a fur muff ...

My Fair Lady harkened in a romantic revival that also could be seen in pale lipstick shades; floral print silks; floating fabrics; soft, pale furs such as chinchilla; and feminine froufrou: ribbons, feathers, and lace. The high waistline was kept small by wide sashes, and full skirts remained in fashion but lost their stiffness and numerous petticoats in favor of deep pleats or airy layers of sheer fabric.

Suits also were softer in cut and material by fall 1956, especially for the country and campus, where skirts were cut with more room at the hipline and jackets were often made with bloused backs to give a graceful slouch to the profile. The blouson back was worked into dresses, especially in sheer, drapeable fabrics like crepe chiffon or jersey.

American women were still under the influence of *My Fair Lady*, wearing floral prints and soft, sheer fabrics when Chanel became a hit again in spring 1957. This time, the slim-skirted suits featured loose, buttonless jackets, worn open over patterned silk blouses that matched the jacket lining and were accented with the miles of gold chain that would become classic features of the Chanel suit.

Another classic to be rediscovered and defined in 1957 was the very American shirtwaist: a sportswear basic that worked well for almost any daytime occasion. Against these classics were fads like chiffon cardigans for summer, which gave their wearers just enough protection against the air-conditioned interiors that were becoming more common. Then there was the sack dress.

New York designer Norell showed beltless chemise dresses, but Paris designers Balenciaga and Givenchy went to the extreme in fall 1957 with the creation of the unfitted, blouson sheath dress dubbed the "sack." Making women look like giant sleeved almonds, the shapeless dresses were intended to be worn with high heels and hemlines just below the knee, a full three inches shorter than the previous season, to feature shapely legs. However, the sack dress was unbecoming on most women, even if they sported great legs. Full skirts were exempt from the sack-shaped bodice, but showed influences, especially with skirts arranged into deep folds and tapered or gathered hems to create oval or spherical shapes variously called "egg," "melon," and "balloon" skirts.

The streamlined, rocket-ship silhouette created by the shapeless sack dress continued into 1958. More successful variations on the sack included fitting the front but draping or letting the back hang free. Some designers offered belts or sashes for the wearer to define her waist if she wanted. Others veiled a fitted sheath with an unfitted sheer overdress, especially in

HUTZLER'S

New school of thought on late-day lines: slim and sinuous silk crepe dramatized with draping. Dress and dinner hat by

Ben Reig

Ours alone in

Baltimore

Advertisement for Ben Reig from *Vogue* magazine, October 1, 1956, showing the *My Fair Lady* effect of late Edwardian-era styles upon American fashion in 1956 and 1957.

tent shapes, borrowed from Yves St. Laurent's spring 1958 "trapeze" collection. Young women made the loose outline a success for spring 1958, but the success was short lived. American designers found a solution by drawing in the loose silhouette with a high waistline; Paris autumn collections also looked to high waists. Many dresses, especially evening and cocktail dresses, were designed as part of an ensemble with a matching coat in a trapeze outline with a swinging hemline and large collar.

Fashion excesses quieted down in 1959. The waistline was redefined, and slim or full skirts tapered slightly toward the hemline to accentuate female curves. The waistline was often the entire area from under the bosom to the top of the hip, wrapped by a wide cummerbund sash. Chanel continued to

Grenelle-Estévez coral-colored silk satin dress in an extreme version of the sack style, fall 1957–spring 1958.

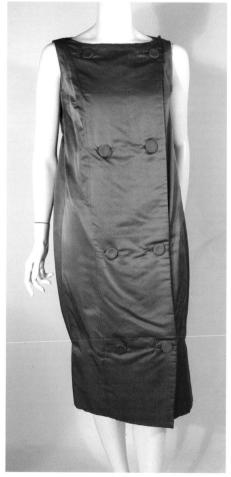

wield influence in suit design; her casual, open jackets now featured contrasting binding and brass buttons, features that were shamelessly adapted and copied by Seventh Avenue. And as the decade came to a close, the more modern, streamlined silhouette that could be found in the long, narrow evening dresses became the standard of the coming decade, displacing the bouffant evening gowns that had been in fashion since the late 1940s.

Rose print silk taffeta balloon dress, by Sara Fredericks, c. 1956–58. Sara Fredericks was a luxury-clothing boutique that carried imported European and American designer fashions, as well as a signature line created by various designers over the years.

Hannah Troy

DESIGNERS AND MANUFACTURERS OF HIGH FASHION

IN THE 1950s, American designers were starting to come into their own—and to be recognized by industry insiders as well as consumers. A number of designers shaped the way women dressed.

Abe Schrader was born in Poland and worked his way up the ladder of the fashion business, establishing his own New York Seventh Avenue ready-to-wear business in 1952. Belle Saunders was his head designer. In 1958, his son, Mort Schrader, created an eponymous division for young women's styles.

Adele Simpson began working at the Mary Lee dress company in New York in 1942, and created her first eponymous line of fashion in 1944. She purchased the company in 1949 and renamed it Adele Simpson Inc.

Gilbert Adrian, who went by just "Adrian," was a prominent Hollywood costume designer for such movies as *The Philadelphia Story*, *The Wizard of Oz*, and *The Women* before he opened his own fashion house during World War II and sold a line of clothes through select department stores across the country. He closed his business in 1952.

Anna Miller was a New York manufacturer of high-end fashions, as was her brother Maurice Rentner. Bill Blass became the head designer at Miller in the early 1950s. After Maurice Rentner died in 1958, Anna Miller merged the companies and placed Blass in charge of design.

Anne Fogarty began designing for the New York firm of Margot Inc. in 1950, where she received a Coty award in 1951 and a Neiman Marcus award in 1952 for her work. She also designed for the Youth Guild during the 1950s, a line founded in 1948 for the teen market. In 1959, she wrote the book *Wife Dressing*, which provided advice on how to dress. In 1962, she opened her own design house, Anne Fogarty Inc.

Arnold Scaasi (born Arnold Isaacs) landed his first design job assisting Charles James in 1953. He designed his first freelance ready-to-wear collection in New York in 1956 and received a Coty award in 1958 and Neiman Marcus award in 1959.

Ben Barrack was a New York firm that specialized in midpriced clothes

Opposite:
Advertisement for
Hannah Troy from
Vogue magazine,
November 15,
1959.

Advertisement for
Adele Simpson
from *Vogue*
magazine,
September 1, 1951.

Advertisement
for coats by
Adrian, from
Vogue magazine,
September 15,
1950.

"THE COAT"
BY **ADRIAN**

for petites designed by Ben's wife Florence. The company
was founded before 1940 and closed in 1969.

Ben Reig was founded in New York in 1929 and was
best known for elevating cotton into a status fashion fabric.
During the 1950s, the designers at Reig were Omar Kiam
until 1954, and then Edward Beckham from 1954 until
1960, followed by Eva Rosencrans the following year.
The company closed in 1973.

Ben Zuckerman was born in Romania and worked his
way up through the garment industry, literally starting as

a floor sweeper. He began a tailoring firm in 1925 that became his eponymous New York company in 1950. He received a Neiman Marcus award in 1951 and two Coty awards, in 1952 and 1958. Harry Shacter was the designer at Zuckerman from 1950 until the firm closed in 1968.

Bonnie Cashin returned to New York in 1949 after a career as a Hollywood costume designer. While working for Adler and Adler, a coat manufacturer, she received both a Neiman Marcus

Advertisement for Anna Miller, from *Vogue* magazine, January 1, 1951.

IF IT'S UNEXPECTED,

EXPECT IT FROM

Anne Fogarty

The deep V front and back ... plus those famous Fogarty cachets: the minimum waist, the maximum skirt, the unexpected fabric —this multicolor quilted cotton by Bates. Sizes 5 to 15. About $35.

Advertisement for Anne Fogarty, from *Vogue* magazine, February 1, 1952.

Opposite:
Green silk taffeta
cocktail dress by
Ceil Chapman,
c. 1957

Right:
Advertisement for
Ben Barrack, from
Vogue magazine,
February 1, 1956.

Below:
Advertisement
for Branell, from
Vogue magazine,
January 1, 1957.

award and a Coty award in 1950. In 1951, Cashin established herself as a freelance designer, and in 1953 she began designing leather clothing for Sills and Company, where she became known for using leather and unusual findings such as industrial zippers, dog leash clasps, and metal toggles. Later, in the 1960s, she created handbag designs for Coach.

Branell was a Seventh Avenue New York fashion house founded by Al Blumenstein. Their coats, suits, and dresses were made for clients with conservative tastes. The company was in business from 1939 until 1971.

Ceil Chapman specialized in midpriced cocktail and evening clothes. She was a favorite with Broadway stars and Hollywood celebrities and even made Elizabeth Taylor's wedding gown for her marriage to Nicky Hilton in 1950. She closed her shop in 1965.

Charles James was born in Britain but worked in the United Kingdom, France, and the United States. He did his best work in the early 1950s, when he had a roster of American socialites who patiently waited for their couture gowns. James received a Neiman Marcus award in 1953 and two Coty awards, in 1950 and 1954. A line of ready-to-wear for Samuel Winston in the mid-1950s ended in a lawsuit with James losing the case—and most of his money. James closed his New York couture business in 1958.

Christian Dior New York opened in October 1948, with Christian Dior himself travelling to New York twice a year with the American collections. By 1951, business had grown too large to handle from across the Atlantic, and manufacturing was shifted to Seventh Avenue in New York. The designs continued to come from Paris until 1961. Dior New York was strictly a ready-to-wear manufacturer that sold to a select group of high-end department and specialty-clothing stores across the United States.

Dan Millstein created adaptations of Paris suits as well as original designs by his in-house New York designers. Marilyn Monroe was married to Joe DiMaggio in 1954 wearing a Millstein suit.

David Hart (born David Hartog) founded his New York business by 1953. His designer,

Frank Perullo, created midpriced dressy fashions for high-end department stores like Saks Fifth Avenue and Lord & Taylor. The company closed in 1963.

Davidow was one of New York's oldest clothing firms still operating in the 1950s. Famous for exquisitely tailored coats and suits, including near exact copies of Chanel, the company went out of business in about 1973.

Advertisement for Christian Dior New York, from *Vogue* magazine, September 1, 1951.

Advertisement for Davidow, from *Vogue* magazine, August 1, 1951.

Don Loper was a Hollywood fashion designer who made clothes for actresses in the 1950s, including Gracie Allen and Lucille Ball, who featured his fashions in a 1955 episode of *I Love Lucy* titled "The Fashion Show" that has Lucy modelling a tweed suit when she has a severe sunburn.

Donald Brooks began designing store windows at the New York department store Lord & Taylor in 1950, where his talents were spotted. Soon after, he began designing collections. In 1958, he received a Coty award for his evening clothes, and later that year, he moved to Townley Frocks after Claire McCardell's passing.

Dorothy O'hara started as a costume designer but found more success as a fashion designer to the stars. She also designed under the Fashion Forecast, Inc. label.

Edith Small opened her business in Los Angeles in 1945 and was known for her high-quality fabrics. The company was closed in 1965.

Eisenberg was a New York wholesale manufacturer of high-end ladies' clothing since 1914 but ceased making clothes in 1958 in order to concentrate on jewelry. Their designer in the 1950s was Irma Kirby.

Elizabeth Arden was born Florence Nightingale Graham near Toronto, Canada. After moving to New York in 1909, she opened a beauty salon, and eventually expanded into clothing. She briefly employed Charles James but fired him and instead hired Ferdinando Sarmi as her in-house designer from 1951 to 1959. Oscar de la Renta replaced Sarmi in 1959.

Emma Domb was a San Francisco-based company that

Advertisement for Dorothy O'hara, from *Vogue* magazine, March 1, 1956.

Advertisement for Eisenberg, from *Vogue* magazine, August 1, 19

Advertisement for
a Geoffrey Beene-
designed suit for
Harmay, from
Vogue magazine,
August 15, 1954.

Silk oyster satin
and lace dress,
by Harvey Berin,
c. 1956–57.

specialized in evening and event clothes such as prom dresses and wedding gowns.

Hannah Troy used wartime statistical research on American women's sizes to invent the petite size for shorter-waisted women. She manufactured petite ready-to-wear in New York for the best department stores in America. George Saman was the designer in the late 1950s, when the label became known for its adaptations of Italian designs.

Harmay was launched in 1949 in New York and soon after hired a young Geoffrey Beene as their designer. Beene remained at the conservative suit and dress manufacturer until 1957 when Harmay fired him for designing loose-fitting chemise styles. Beene went on to the new company of Teal Traina in 1958, where he stayed until going out on his own in 1963.

Harvey Berin appointed his sister-in-law Karen Stark as his company's designer in 1945. She received a Coty award in 1952 and was known for her dressy but conservative New York-made, Paris-inspired fashions. The company closed in 1970.

Advertisement for Hattie Carnegie, from *Vogue* magazine, March 1, 1959.

Hattie Carnegie expanded her business from a millinery into a boutique in 1919 and bought Paris designer clothes to resell and make adaptations for her New York shop. She also employed designers to create couture and ready-to-wear clothes, but never gave them credit on her label. By the time of her death in 1956, Carnegie's name had become synonymous with American good taste. The custom salon continued after her death until 1965, and the business finally closed in 1976.

Helen Rose came to Hollywood to work as a costume designer in 1943, but like many costumers also designed a line of fashion wear on the side in the 1950s. She retired in 1968.

Helena Barbieri was a New York-based designer of evening dresses and formal gowns from 1949 into the 1960s.

Helga was established in San Francisco by Robert and Helga Oppenheimer in 1947, with Robert managing the business while Helga designed the dressy and evening clothes the company became known for. They moved to Los Angeles in the early 1950s.

Herbert Sondheim was a fixture in the organization and promotion of New York fashion when he wasn't busy overseeing the operation of his company, which was known for making dressy high-end fashions since 1923. The company closed in 1964. Herbert was the father of composer Stephen Sondheim.

Howard Greer had already owned a couture business in Los Angeles for nearly twenty years when he added ready-to-wear in 1947. He became known for dinner dresses specifically designed with interesting necklines to look good while seated at the table. He retired in 1962.

Silk taffeta cocktail dress by Herbert Sondheim, c. 1956–57.

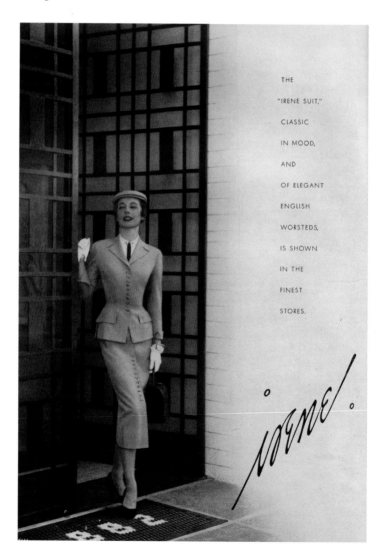

THE

"IRENE SUIT,"

CLASSIC

IN MOOD,

AND

OF ELEGANT

ENGLISH

WORSTEDS,

IS SHOWN

IN THE

FINEST

STORES.

Advertisement for Irene, from *Vogue* magazine, April 15, 1954.

Irene Lentz worked as a Hollywood costumer during the 1940s, but began designing a line of high-end ready-to-wear suits for select department stores beginning in 1947. She designed under the name "Irene" until her death in 1962.

Jablow was a high-end New York manufacturer of suits, dresses, and coats owned by Arthur Jablow but founded by his father George. The firm's lead designer during the 1950s was David Kidd, who often interpreted designs by Balenciaga and Chanel. The company closed in 1966.

Advertisement for Jablow, from *Vogue* magazine, September 1, 1954.

James Galanos worked at several Seventh Avenue firms in New York before opening his Los Angeles fashion house in 1951. Galanos received a Neiman Marcus award in 1954 and Coty awards in 1954, 1956, and 1959. He became especially known for his chiffon evening wear and is generally recognized as one of the leading designers of American fashion in the 1950s.

Jane Derby specialized in making mature women's fashions, including three- and four-piece suits and evening wear for her New York firm. She received both a Neiman Marcus and a Coty award in 1951.

Jo Copeland became the designer of Pattullo Modes in 1938. Her last trip to Paris was in 1947 because she didn't want to be influenced by Paris styles. Her American fashions were nonetheless high-end designs for society women.

John Moore worked for different New York manufacturers before opening his own business in 1963. He received a Coty award for evening wear for Mattie Talmack's label in 1953. He also designed dresses to order, including the dress Marilyn Monroe wore at her marriage to Arthur Miller in 1956.

Joseph Halpert, known for elegant afternoon and dinner dresses since 1930, contracted Parisian couturier Jacques Fath to design two collections a year under the Halpert label from fall 1949 to spring 1954, shortly before Fath died. Joseph Halpert liquidated his New York company at the end of 1954.

Lanz was originally a traditional folkwear shop in Austria when a branch was opened in New York. In 1947, a ready-to-wear manufacturer for Lanz was established in California, but after it was sold to Werner and Nornie Scharff in 1952, the company moved further away from traditional Austrian designs with each passing year.

Larry Aldrich had been a New York manufacturer since 1927. In 1957, Marie McCarthy, who had been at Aldrich for fourteen years, was named head designer.

Leslie Morris designed made-to-order fashions at the New York clothier Bergdorf Goodman from 1928 until 1967 and received a Coty award in 1957. Bergdorf Goodman closed its couture salon in 1969.

Advertisement for Lanz, from *Vogue* magazine, September 1, 1959.

Opposite: Silk print chiffon late-day dress, by James Galanos, c. 1957–58.

Advertisement for
Larry Aldrich, from
Vogue magazine,
February 1, 1952.

Right: Lilli Ann
red wool and silk
blend suit, c. 1951.

Lilli Ann was founded in San Francisco in 1933 by Adolph Schuman, who named the company for his wife, Lillian. Schuman went to France to promote San Francisco manufacturers in the late 1940s and sought out French and Italian woolens for his exuberantly styled high-fashion suits and coats.

Luis Estévez was born in Cuba and trained in Paris before he started designing in 1955 under the New York-based Grenelle-Estévez label. He received a Coty award in 1956. His label closed in 1968, and Estévez went on to freelance design afterward.

Mainbocher was the first American haute couturier who opened in Paris in 1930, but he returned to the United States in 1940. He worked from his atelier on 57th Street in New York, where he designed costumes for Broadway and couture for society clients, until he closed in 1971.

Martini was a New York dress company that made adaptations of Paris designs. The in-house designers Shannon Rodgers and Jerry Silverman left in 1959 to establish their own label.

Maurice Rentner was known for quality suits and dresses. After his death in 1958, the New York-based company merged with his sister Anna Miller's company, and Bill Blass became the designer.

Miss Elliette was owned and designed by Canadian-born Elliette Ellis, who started her own line in 1952. She made feminine, midpriced chiffon dinner and cocktail dresses from her Los Angeles-based company.

Mollie Parnis designed shirtwaist dresses and straight-skirt suits with boxy jackets that were popular with First

Above:
Luis Estévez
feather brocade
taffeta evening
dress, autumn
1956.

Far left:
Advertisement
for Martini, from
Vogue magazine,
September 15,
1953.

Left:
Advertisement for
Maurice Rentner,
from *Vogue*
magazine,
September 1, 1957.

Advertisement for
Mollie Parnis, from
Vogue magazine,
November 15,
1951.

Lady Mamie Eisenhower. In April 1955, Mollie Parnis made news when Mrs. Eisenhower and another woman wore the same Mollie Parnis print dress to the same reception.

Monte-Sano & Pruzan was founded as a custom tailoring shop in New York, and by the 1950s was producing ready-to-wear suits and coats. Vincent Monte-Sano received a Neiman Marcus award in 1952, the same year Jacques Tiffeau began as designer for the firm. Tiffeau received backing from Monte-Sano & Pruzan for his own venture, Tiffeau & Busch, in 1958.

Mr. Mort was founded in New York in 1952 by Mortimer Goldman. The company produced midpriced, high-fashion dresses. Stan Herman became the designer at Mr. Mort in 1959.

Nettie Rosenstein was a New York designer known for evening clothes and for making both of Mamie Eisenhower's inaugural gowns. In 1957, Rosenstein created a sportswear line but shuttered her clothing lines in 1961.

Oleg Cassini designed his first line of fashions in New York in 1948. He boasted that he created the Grace Kelly look around the time that he was dating her in the early 1950s, and he later went on to become the official couturier for First Lady Jacqueline Kennedy in 1960.

Originala was a high-end Seventh Avenue suit and coat house founded by Louis Bader and run by his two sons, Nat and Irving Bader. The company went public in 1961.

Pauline Trigère was born and trained in Paris before immigrating to the United States, where she opened her own company in 1942. She designed for and managed her New York high-fashion business with a small staff for nearly sixty years. She received a Neiman Marcus award in 1950 and Coty awards in 1951 and 1959.

Peck & Peck was one of New York's oldest firms, established by brothers Edgar and George Peck in 1888 as a hosiery firm. By the 1950s, they were known as a quality clothing brand that was sold through their own chain of seventy-eight stores across the United States.

Peggy Hunt developed the Collegienne department at Bullocks Wilshire in Los Angeles. Under the Peggy Hunt label, her specialty was evening and cocktail dresses.

Philip Hulitar had been the custom designer at Bergdorf Goodman since 1935 before opening his own New York business in 1949, specializing in evening clothes. He retired in 1964.

Rudolf was founded by Max Cory Rudolf but flourished under his son Charlie Rudolf after he took over the business in the late 1940s. In the 1950s, Givenchy designed a line of dresses for Rudolf Gowns.

Sally Milgrim was the head designer of Milgrims, a New York store founded in the 1920s that had branches in Chicago, Cleveland, Detroit, and elsewhere. Milgrim also designed a line of ready-to-wear under the label "Salymil" until she retired in 1960.

Advertisement for Mr. Mort, from *Harper's Bazaar* magazine, November 1958.

Advertisement for Samuel Winston, from *Vogue* magazine, September 1, 1957.

Advertisement for Seymour Fox, from *Vogue* magazine, September 15, 1951.

Samuel Winston was a Seventh Avenue manufacturer producing several lines under different labels. In 1955, Winston entered into an agreement with Charles James to produce a line of clothes, but the arrangement ended badly after a couple of seasons.

Seymour Fox was a highly regarded Seventh Avenue coat and suit manufacturer founded in about 1950.

Seymour Jacobson founded his eponymous New York company in 1949 to produce couture-style cocktail and evening dresses. Afternoon dresses were made under the Jaymor label.

Sophie for Saks was Sophie Gimble, the wife of Adam Gimbel, president of Saks Fifth Avenue. Sophie was the in-house designer for the "Salon Moderne" dressmaking department at Saks, which operated from 1931 until 1969 and also carried Paris couture originals.

Advertisement for Seymour Jacobson, from *Vogue* magazine, February 1, 1956.

suzy perette!

"Good Fortune"...Taking its name from the authentic Chinese character brilliants that light Suzy Perette's carbon spill of liquid rayon velvet. $29.95
Sizes 8 to 16 — Third Floor

only at *Russeks*

NEW YORK · BROOKLYN
CROSS COUNTY · CHICAGO

Advertisement for Suzy Perette, from *Vogue* magazine, August 15, 1955.

Advertisement for Swansdown, from *Vogue* magazine, April 1, 1952.

Advertisement for Traina-Norell, from *Vogue* magazine, March 15, 1958.

Suzy Perette was a line of midpriced high-fashion dresses often adapted from Parisian designs, especially Dior. The line was a division of Lombardy Frocks, created by Max Blauner in the late 1940s, trademarking the name in 1954. "Gigi Young" was a less expensive line from the same company that debuted in the late 1950s.

Swansdown was a Seventh Avenue firm that specialized in high-end copies of Paris-designed suits. The House of Swansdown was at their height of success in the early 1950s.

Traina-Norell was a partnership between Anthony Traina and designer Norman Norell, who received two Coty awards, in 1951 and 1956. After Anthony Traina died in 1958, Norell continued to work under the label until he formed his own company in 1960.

Valentina Sanina Schlee was always known by just her first name. The Russian-born designer created couture originals for New York socialites and Hollywood stars from her 67th Street atelier from 1940 until she closed in 1957.

William Travilla began his career as a costume designer in the 1940s. His most famous work was done for Marilyn Monroe in the films *Gentlemen Prefer Blondes* and *The Seven Year Itch*. He began designing a line of ready-to-wear clothes under his own name in the late 1950s.

Yaga was the custom dressmaker Lala Pawlowicz. She began her New York business in the early 1950s and made semiannual trips to Europe to buy fabric and to "take the pulse of fashion."

Zelinka-Matlick was a Seventh Avenue suit and coat house founded by David Zelinka and Max Matlick in 1935. They became known for their well-tailored interpretations of Paris suits.

Advertisement
for Travilla, from
Vogue magazine,
November 15,
1959.

Left: Balloon-skirt
silk chiffon dress
with high-waisted
satin belt, by Yaga,
c. 1958.

SUBURBIA, U.S.A. INC.
GOUTURIER ORIGINALS

Multiple exposures A wonderful way to troop the colors in COLOR GUARD by Suburbia, U.S.A....a whole colle of coordinates that combine basic strategy with new tactics. Top brass jacket in pure wool flannel, $40. Crescent yoke silk blend shirt, $15. slim skirt in flannel, saddle-stitched with gold p——, $20. All in flag red, U.S. navy, saddle w——, l——as-brass or black. Sizes 8 to 18. Ca COLOR GUARD coordinated originals at the finest stores everywhere; or write to Suburbia, U.S.A., Inc., 525 Seventh Avenue, New York 18,

OFF THE RACK—FROM SEVENTH AVENUE TO HOLLYWOOD

COUTURE WAS THE ESSENCE of Paris's fashion industry, but couture did not carry the same weight in America. The best-known American couturiers of the 1950s worked out of New York: Valentina, Charles James, and Mainbocher, as well as the custom salons at Elizabeth Arden, Hattie Carnegie, Saks Fifth Avenue, Bergdorf Goodman, and Henri Bendel. But these businesses slowly lost clientele during the decade. Valentina closed in 1957, James in 1958, and all other custom salons closed during the 1960s, leaving only Mainbocher still in business (until 1971).

Ready-to-wear was New York's strength and its largest industry in the 1950s. Many of the city's leading garment manufacturers had started as family businesses founded in the early years of the century by Jewish immigrants from Central Europe. New York had the perfect combination of access to skilled labor, domestic and imported materials, support industries (from advertising to publishing), and markets (from influential socialites to the buying offices of leading department stores). The New York garment trade also was a leader in labor organization and brand protection.

In 1940, the New York Dress Institute (NYDI) was formed as an association between garment unions and clothing manufacturers to promote New York as the center of the American fashion industry. To promote the NYDI, a best-dressed list was created by fashion publicist Eleanor Lambert, who in 1943 also began the first Press Week (the forerunner of Fashion Week). The mandate of the NYDI shifted over the years into an organization that standardized release dates for seasonal collections and organized Press Week. In 1953, the unions decided the organization was too regional for their membership. The New York Dress Institute was reinvented as the New York Couture Group. Membership was open to New York-based manufacturers of quality ready-to-wear suits, coats, and dresses that retailed for more than $80, who also paid an annual membership fee of $1,000. From 1953 until 1965, the Couture Group controlled New York's high-end fashion industry. Infighting ultimately led to dwindling membership, however, which forced a merger with the American Fashion Business Council in early 1966.

Opposite:
Advertisement for Suburbia, U.S.A. The company made clothes by various designers, including John Harberger, better known as the milliner Mr. John. As the name of the company attests, its target audience was the suburban woman. Advertisement from *Vogue*, November 15, 1959.

37

New York wasn't the country's only fashion mecca. In California, the fashion industry grew rapidly between 1920 and 1950, almost entirely because of the film industry. Every studio had a bevy of actresses to be dressed in the latest elegant fashions for photo shoots and red carpet events. The film industry also needed designers who could anticipate where fashion was headed in order to avoid outmoded looks in films when they were released a year after production. Dressmakers, tailors, shoemakers, milliners, embroiderers, and other fashion professionals flocked to Hollywood during the 1930s and 1940s. By the 1950s, many costume designers had started a fashion line on the side or switched completely to fashion design. Some of the most popular among them were Adrian, Irene, Howard Greer, William Travilla, Oleg Cassini, Bonnie Cashin, Dorothy O'hara, and Helen Rose.

California was also influential in promoting sportswear. The temperate, sunny climate, expansive beaches, and poolside lifestyle enjoyed by glamorous film stars became the envy of American women. When not attending premieres or dining at the latest nightspots, film stars were depicted wearing sportswear separates that suited the casual California lifestyle.

Sportswear no longer meant clothes intended only for sporting activity. In the 1920s, Paris designers Chanel and Patou borrowed clothes from the tennis court, beach, and stables to create a casual look for young, modern women. The sporty fashions were practical, and they were successfully

"Designed together" separates including slacks, sweaters, and jumpers, from Montgomery Ward catalogue, fall 1954.

translated by American mass production in the form of easy-fitting sweaters, skirts, blouses, and jackets. American women were receptive to the casually styled clothes, and sportswear became the strength of American design and manufacturing. As the population moved to the suburbs in the 1950s, women needed a fashion that, like their environs, was halfway between town and country, and sportswear filled that need perfectly.

Higher clothing costs in the early 1950s inspired sportswear manufacturers to make "designed together" separates: color-coordinated flannel, tartan, and velveteen jackets, skirts, waistcoats, and slacks that could be mixed and matched with a variety of blouses and sweaters for maximum use. Separates were not just for daytime: glamorous velvet and satin skirts and tops for at-home entertaining and cocktail-through-dinner wear became à la mode at the start of the decade.

When full skirts caught on in the United States in 1951, four years after their debut in Paris, the style was most popular as a sportswear separate. Felt or cotton skirts, paired with sleeveless blouses or sweaters and worn with wide, elasticized "cinch" belts (introduced by Schiaparelli in spring 1952), were popular with American women. The skirts ranged from almost straight, hanging pleated styles to full silhouettes with hemlines wider than a circle's radius, held out by numerous petticoats.

Trousers also grew in favor throughout the decade, especially in tapered-to-the-ankle slacks dubbed

Modernist print cotton skirt, brown leather belt, and cashmere wool-blend sweater set with gold metal sweater clip, c. late 1950s.

Felt skirt with musical note appliqués and patches referring to leading singers of the late 1950s, including Perry Como and Elvis "The King" Presley. Presley was first referred to as the King of Rock and Roll in October 1956.

Printed cotton corduroy TV pajamas or "at-home" hostess trouser set, unlabeled, c. mid-1950s.

"toreadors" by 1953. A new type of outfit appeared in 1950 that embraced trousers: TV pajamas. This type of at-home lounging outfit of tapered slacks in velveteen, satin, or corduroy with a tailored tunic top was designed to offer glamorous comfort as well as respectability in case company popped by. As the decade progressed, the favorite at-home costume consisted of tapered trousers with a sweater top. By the end of the decade, younger women took the look to the extreme, choosing bulky sweaters over skin-tight pants or dancer's tights.

Knitwear offered economical alternatives for every occasion throughout the 1950s. Turtleneck sweaters became a hit for wearing under a suit or jumper, instead of a blouse. For evening glamor, dressy, wing-sleeved sweaters and cardigans embroidered with beads, sequins, and fake jewels gained popularity throughout the decade and even took the place of evening wraps for cool evenings.

After New York and California, St. Louis, Missouri, and its environs was the third largest manufacturing center in the United States in the 1950s. In the August 1, 1950, issue, *Vogue* magazine reported: "St. Louis is made up of a group of manufacturers who generally concentrate on the figures, tastes, and finances of the young." It all began in 1934, when Irving Sorger, of the St. Louis department store Kline's, surveyed his female customers and found that young women wanted clothes that better suited their youth, in both fit and style. The younger figure was leaner, less curvaceous, and generally shorter waisted. Sorger identified this group as the "junior" market, and St. Louis soon became the manufacturing hub of junior ready-to-wear fashions.

A *New York Times* article from March 17, 1951, claimed there were 115 clothing manufacturers in the St. Louis area, and about ninety nationally known labels. Most of these lines were designed by young women who graduated from the fashion arts program of St. Louis's Washington University.

Most St. Louis-area manufacturers opted to use fanciful names for their lines. For example, Lang-Kohn, which was known as L&K, created a junior line under the "homonyistic" label "Ellen Kaye." The J. A. & M. B. Kelly Company (founded by brothers John Alexander Kelly and Marion Burton Kelly) used a contraction of the owners' names for their line "Jo-Burt Juniors." R. Lowenbaum Manufacturing made "Jon McCauley" (sportswear) and "Minx Modes." Alex Carafiol Inc. made junior clothes under the label "Frances Dexter," and "Connie Carter" was the junior line made by Weinstock Manufacturing Company.

Brands and labels were nothing new to fashion. The American garment industry had relied upon brand recognition since the late nineteenth century. Some early brands, like Florsheim shoes, were advertised in nationally distributed magazines to build brand recognition even before the shoes were available everywhere. Mascots, logos, slogans, testimonials, celebrity endorsements—all of these techniques were used to sell garments, especially those that did not rely on design but rather measurable qualities including durability, comfort, and ease of care. Brands such as Swirl dresses, Keds shoes, and Maidenform brassieres were successful across America, regardless of who retailed them.

The opposite of the brands made intentionally for national appeal were styles that developed regionally, but they too were becoming iconic American fashions in the 1950s. Floral printed Aloha shirts, sarongs, and muumuus were made in and around Honolulu but could be found as far away as the beaches of Florida. Cowboy boots, originally black leather cavalry boots in the late 1860s, were honed in style and utility until by the 1950s, colorful, tooled leather cowboy boots could be found at barbeques and square dances from coast to coast. Similarly, Western wear, including squaw dresses, embroidered shirts with pearly snaps, and bolo ties, were made by manufacturers across the Southwest, but were worn from California to Connecticut.

Perhaps the most ubiquitous American fashion was blue jeans. The most famous manufacturer of the style was San Francisco clothier Levi Strauss & Co. They became famous for making dungarees with riveted stress points, which they started manufacturing in 1873 for cowboys and lumberjacks. By the 1930s, their work pants were known for their durability, an asset during the Depression for farmers and factory workers. Levi's designed a cut for women in 1935, but it wasn't

The Brand Names Foundation Inc. was created with an ethical mission to uphold the prestige and value of identifiable merchandise. Brand-name goods had an innate guarantee of quality and certified the makers would stand behind their product. Advertisement to "Buy Brand Names" campaign, from *Vogue* magazine, October 15, 1959.

Smart Shoppers ... Buy by BRAND NAME

a **BRAND NAME** *is a maker's reputation*

Dressing for comfort was on the rise in the 1950s. Denim and blouse casual attire from Montgomery Ward catalogue, fall 1951.

until after World War II when teenagers started wearing blue jeans for casual occasions that denim culture took off. When Marlon Brando and James Dean donned jeans for their rebel roles, the look became iconic for the decade.

Teenaged girls wore jeans cut to fit their curves, with high waists and side zippers, and rolled hems to reveal another icon of the decade: saddle shoes. The two-toned shoes available in white with navy, brown, or black had soared in popularity in the mid-1930s and were still in fashion in the early 1950s. But as the decade progressed, young women began to prefer toe-cleavage-baring ballerina pumps, tennis shoes, "Weejuns" (a brand of slip-on loafer), and "Hush Puppies" (a brand-name pig suede ankle boot with crepe rubber soles that was an instant hit when introduced in 1958).

Despite the popularity of sportswear and the new suburban casual lifestyle, there was still a reserved, sometimes prudish, attitude toward certain fashions in America. While buxom European beauties like Brigitte Bardot and Ursula Andress were making bikinis acceptable at Cannes and St. Tropez, the only place to see a belly-button-baring bikini in the United States was in a girlie magazine. One-piece swimsuits dominated American beachwear throughout the decade. Looking like evening gowns from the waist up, the tops were often strapless and elasticized to flatter the hourglass figure. Bottoms ranged from puffed and skirted styles to sporty boy-cut shorts. The addition of a matching over-skirt or wrap transformed bathing suits into play-clothes suitable for lounging poolside. In the end, it was the overtly wholesome Sandra Dee who sported a modest bikini in *Gidget*, the 1959 film that heralded a wave of California beach movies brimming with bikini-clad teens, that would change American attitudes about sexuality and fashion in the coming decade.

The only measurable challenge to mainstream fashion in the 1950s was coming from the counterculture Beats. The media made light of the movement in 1957 by coining the term "Beatnik," adding the Russian suffix from Sputnik to Beat. Sprouting from a group of New York writers in the late 1940s, the Beat generation swelled into an international movement that embraced atonal jazz, black coffee, free love, existentialism, scruffy beards, dark glasses, berets, and sandals. Converts to the movement could be found from Greenwich Village to Haight Ashbury, and as far afield as the left bank of Paris and the coffee houses of Chelsea, London. Toward the end of the decade, the movement became more politicized, declaring antimaterialism as a way of life, and many Beats became active in antiwar protests and civil rights. The Beat generation was a symptom of a changing society that would explode in the coming "youthquake" culture of the 1960s.

Cotton dress with print of crabs in fishing net, made by "Paradise Fashions," Hawaii, c. 1955.

TRIBAL PRINTS

stirring as jungle drums

vibrant as tropical plumage

in better dresses and by-the-yard

cotton fabrics by

Peter Pan

guaranteed ✿ fast color

DESIGNERS AND MANUFACTURERS OF EVERYDAY FASHIONS

JUST AS AMERICAN DESIGNERS of American high-end fashion shaped the industry in the 1950s, so did designers and manufacturers of casual and ready-to-wear clothing. And, as with the couture designers, a number became easily recognized names.

One of the most important and successful designers of the 1940s and '50s, Addie Masters specialized in California casual clothing. Her first success was hostess pants.

Agnes Barrett was one of the pioneers of the California look and is credited with inventing the broomstick skirt (a skirt made up of gathered tiers).

Alex Colman's wife Sade was making blouses in 1949 under the label "Alex Colman—California." The company went on to produce sportswear coordinates and California casual dresses with Sade Colman's sister, Blanche Lefton, as head designer.

Alice of California was founded by Krist Gunderson, who by 1947 was operating a factory in San Francisco that advertised "… colorful, casual, comfortable and Californian" clothes under the "Lady Alice" label.

Alix of Miami made cocktail and dinner dresses with a tropical styling. They also made swimsuits, which were frequently studded with rhinestones. One of the founders was Luther V. Powell, who later worked at Serbin, another Miami clothing manufacturer.

Anne Klein and her husband Ben formed the Junior Sophisticates label in New York in 1948. Anne received a Coty award in 1955 for her sophisticated clothes for young women. After Junior Sophisticates, Anne formed Anne Klein and Company in 1968 but died unexpectedly in 1974, although her company continued on.

B. H. Wragge became known for sportswear separates after Sydney Goldstein bought the New York company in 1931. In the 1950s, Goldstein expanded into dresses and suits for the collegiate customer. He received Coty awards in 1952 and 1957.

Bill Atkinson got into fashion by accident when he made a square dance outfit for his wife out of eight bandanna handkerchiefs. In 1950, the

Opposite:
Advertisement for Carolyn Schnurer from *Vogue* magazine, January 1, 1951.

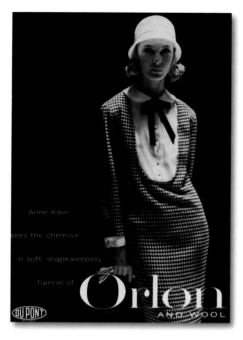

Above left:
Advertisement for
Orlon by Dupont,
illustrated with a
chemise dress by
Anne Klein, from
Vogue magazine,
February 1, 1958.

Above right:
Advertisement
for Acrilan
sportswear
separates by
Bill Atkinson,
from *Vogue*,
August 1, 1956.

company Glen of Michigan began to manufacture Bill Atkinson's casual sportswear designs.

Carlye Dress Company was one of the more famous junior dress houses in St. Louis, from 1938 to 1966 when it was bought out by Leslie Fay. The designer in the early 1950s was Louise Mulligan.

Carolyn Schnurer and her husband Bert formed the Carolyn Schnurer label in the late 1940s, making sundresses, cover-ups, bathing suits, casual party dresses, and some evening wear, often from exotic printed cotton textiles. The label closed in the late 1950s.

Ceeb of Miami was the label of the Miami Sportswear Company. Incorporated in 1946 by Mr. and Mrs. C. B. Brasington and Mr. and Mrs. W. T. Rose, the company was known for their Florida-inspired looks. They made swimsuits, sunsuits, shorts, and slacks sets.

Claire McCardell was a pioneer of American sportswear under the Townley Frocks label, where she worked most of her career. Corset hook closures and wrap-and-tie dresses were her signature styles. McCardell received a Coty award after she died in March 1958.

Cole of California began as the swimsuit division of a knitting mill, becoming famous for its glamorous swim and poolside wear by Margit Felligi.

David Crystal was a men's and women's sportswear manufacturer that bought the Izod name in 1938. In 1952, Crystal licensed the Lacoste name and crocodile logo and became famous for producing tennis and country club wear. The company and its licenses were sold in 1968, and today Izod is owned by Phillips Van Heusen, which also owns Tommy Hilfiger, Calvin Klein, and Arrow.

Stripe printed
cotton dress
with corset hook
closures, by Claire
McCardell, c. 1951.

47

Evan-Picone was formed in New York in 1949 as a manufacturer of women's sportswear separates, especially slacks and skirts, by salesman Charles Evans and tailor Joseph Picone. The company was sold in 1962.

Forest City Manufacturing Company was a St. Louis company that originally manufactured cotton housedresses before branching into junior and sportswear lines. By the 1950s, they were producing lines under several brand names: Peg Palmer (est. 1924), Doris Dodson (est. 1936), Carole King (est. 1937), Martha Manning (est. 1939), June Patton (est. 1949), and Glen Echo (est. 1950). In the early 1950s, Alice Topp was the designer for Doris Dodson; Doris Varnum designed Carole King; Marjory Norton designed June Patton; Rhoda Hanson designed Peg Palmer; and Robert Mayes was the designer for Martha Manning, a line of clothes for the mature woman.

Advertisement for Evan-Picone, from *Vogue* magazine, April 1, 1958.

the zebra ensemble...

ANIMAL collection by *Cole* of California

Swimsuit at left, $10.95.
Ensemble at right (2-piece swimsuit, jacket and pants), about $30.
Cotton in zebra, leopard or tiger.

Advertisement for Cole of California, from *Vogue* magazine, April 15, 1954.

Gay Gibson was a fancifully named volume brand (a mass manufacturer of affordable, everyday fashion sold at chain department stores) made by the Gernes Garment Company in Kansas City, Missouri.

Greta Plattry began making crocheted clothing in New York before expanding into sportswear by the 1950s. She became known for colorful cotton print boy-short bathing suits with versatile cover-ups, as well as dirndl-skirted cotton dresses.

Advertisement for Martha Manning, one of the labels produced by Forest City Manufacturing, from *Vogue* magazine, September 1, 1950.

greta plattry Floral streamer print by WAMSUTTA in dacron and cotton blend. No iron, quick drying. Sundress softly pleated, girdled in cotton chiffon. About $30. One piece boy pants swimsuit. About $18, Deck jacket, fitted and banded at the waist. About $12. Adriatic blue, Sand. Sizes 8 to 16.
BEST & CO., New York · Burdine's, Miami, all stores · John Wanamaker, Philadelphia
B. Forman, Rochester · Bullock's, Los Angeles

Wamsutta
WAMSUTTA MILLS
1430 Broadway, New York 18, N. Y.
Division of M. Lowenstein & Sons, Inc.

Advertisement for Greta Plattry, from *Vogue* magazine, January 1, 1957.

be

Completely You

be your own fashion originator...that's
the fun of being Completely You!
Collect separates in Jantzen color
coordinates to mix or match like mad...
in skirts, jackets and pants of Kharaflannel or
Kharaplaid, fine wovens loomed of Kharafleece.
Add color-cued sweaters
of Kharafleece...exclusive blend
of lambswool, Vicara-nylon that's
mothproofed by Mitin®...and the
picture's complete and Completely You!

Jantzen ·
sweaters · separates

Advertisement for
Jantzen Inc., from
Vogue magazine,
September 1, 1954.

Jantzen was founded in 1910 and became famous for knitted bathing suits before the company expanded into sportswear in 1940. In 1954, the company officially changed its name from Jantzen Knitting Mills to Jantzen Inc. to reflect their wider range of garment manufacturing.

Jerry Gilden was a New York maker of midpriced women's ready-to-wear founded in 1945. At peak production in the mid-1950s, when Sayde Weinberg was head designer, Gilden was producing more than a million garments a year and was well known for his inexpensive cotton dresses. The company closed in 1961.

Joan Miller Juniors was a clothing line made by the Rhea Manufacturing Company of Milwaukee, Wisconsin, between 1940 and 1960. Liz Claiborne was one of the designers for the Joan Miller label in the 1950s.

Jonathan Logan was a made-up name for a New York company founded in 1944 by David Schwartz. By the late 1950s, the designers were Dorris Varnum and Jeanne Carr. The firm made youthful midpriced dresses but eventually became a collection of brands including Betty Barclay, a junior line of ready-to-wear dresses, and Butte Knit, established in 1959.

Juli Lynne Charlot had little money and even fewer sewing skills in 1947 when she made a holiday skirt by applying felt Christmas motifs to a homemade felt circle skirt. The result was so successful that she was soon being commissioned to make felt skirts for a Beverly Hills boutique and later for department stores across the United States. Her most popular design was a poodle skirt that became an icon of the era.

Kay Windsor Frocks Co. of Boston created a line of midpriced dresses. In 1954, they made a line of clothes under the label "Private Secretary" in conjunction with a television program of the same name starring Ann Sothern.

Kimberly Knitwear was established by Jack Lazar in 1946 in New York. The company led in the production of wool-blend sweaters and dresses in the early to mid-1950s.

Koret of California was created by Stephanie and Joe Koret in 1939. The company was a leader in the separates market, producing lines with different coordinating pieces.

L'Aiglon was a volume brand since 1919 of easy-to-care-for, stylish, inexpensive dresses made by the Philadelphia company Biberman. During

Advertisement for Jonathan Logan fashions, from *Vogue* magazine, October 1, 1955.

Appliqued felt circle skirt, unlabelled but in the style first designed by Juli Lynne Charlot for Christmas 1947 that became an iconic look for the 1950s.

the 1950s, L'Aiglon dresses were worn by actresses appearing on the soap opera *The Edge of Night*.

Leslie Fay was founded in 1947 by Fred Pomerantz and named for his daughter. Pomerantz used wartime U.S. government statistics of standard measurements of the female figure for uniform manufacturing to successfully manufacturer affordable dresses and sportswear for the mature woman.

Marjorie Montgomery was a California designer who developed the concept of a

playsuit with several pieces that could be adapted into a dress suitable for the street.

Mildred Orrick designed for Anne Fogarty before stepping in at Townley in 1957 to help finish Claire McCardell's last collection after McCardell became ill. Orrick finished her career at Villager, where she designed from the late 1950s into the 1960s.

Nelly de Grab was a New York sportswear separates firm founded by Austrian-born Nelly and Leo de Grab.

Advertisement for Koret of California, from *Vogue* magazine, September 15, 1951.

Advertisement for Kimberly Knitwear, from *Vogue* magazine, October 1, 1955.

Nelly Don, Inc. began as the Donnelly Garment Company, which was founded in Kansas City, Missouri, in 1931. When founder Nell Donnelly Reed retired in 1956, the company was renamed Nelly Don, Inc.

Pat Premo was a California company owned by Bill Schminke and named for his wife, the designer Pat Premo. The company became known for making golf dresses for women who belonged to clubs where slacks and shorts were not allowed.

Advertisement for Nelly de Grab, from *Vogue* magazine, September 15, 1953.

Gather your clan separates!

time to pick your pets from new Pendleton Scotch Tartans! Take this authentic Johnstone, for one...see how gently it's tailored into the timeless Pendleton 49'er jacket...how perfectly it pairs with your tapered trews or slender skirt...and with lady-like vest and cloche to match. It's a flawless hat-to-hemline look that shows you...and everyone...you've picked separates such as only Pendleton looms, designs, tailors...only of precious pure virgin wool!

49'er Jacket 19.95; Skirt 14.95;
Trews 17.95; Vest 9.95; Cloche 6.95

PENDLETON

ALWAYS VIRGIN WOOL *Sportswear*

Advertisement for Pendleton Woolen Mills, from *Vogue* magazine, September 1, 1954.

Advertisement or R&K Originals, from *Vogue* magazine, May 1, 1954.

Opposite: Advertisement for Serbin of Florida, from *Vogue* magazine, April 1, 1958.

Pendleton Woolen Mills of Oregon first made women's clothing in 1949 in the form of the '49er jacket, a plaid wool, hip-length, long-sleeved jacket with wide collar, patch pockets, and shell buttons. The jacket was a huge hit and a watershed piece in the development of sportswear.

Puritan Dress Company was a volume midpriced dress manufacturer. In 1951, they signed Gloria Swanson as a spokeswoman, placing her name on the label of a line of dresses for the mature women called "Forever Young." Swanson continued to promote the brand for thirty years.

R&K Originals was a volume brand of stylish but affordable fashions made in New York for department stores across the country.

Rockmount Ranch Wear was created in Denver, Colorado, by Jack Weil in 1946 and specialized in Western wear. They originated using snaps on Western-style shirts.

Serbin was founded in Cleveland, Ohio, but moved to Miami in 1951. They specialized in cotton frocks advertised with the slogan "Whether urban or suburban, always wear a Serbin."

Sportwhirl was founded by Rubin and Arthur Goodman and was a maker of practical, colorful, and informal separates. The head designer of Sportwhirl starting in 1951 was Jeanne Campbell, who is credited with popularizing sheath dress styles, including the knitted sheath dress in 1955, for which she received a Coty award.

Swirl was a brand of wrap-around cotton dresses and aprons first created by the Philadelphia firm of L. Nachman & Son Co. in 1944. The company relocated to Easley, South Carolina, by 1953.

Tabak was a California sportswear firm that hired Hollywood costume designer Irene Saltern in 1950 as their head designer. Other than briefly designing her own line between 1955 and 1957, Saltern remained at Tabak until 1965.

Teena Paige was a popular line of day and party dresses for teenagers established in 1944 by the Epstein Garment Company of New York. There was no person by the name of Teena Paige.

Thunderbird was a Western-wear fashion company that included Prescott Sportswear founded by Jack Mims in Prescott, Arizona, in 1946.

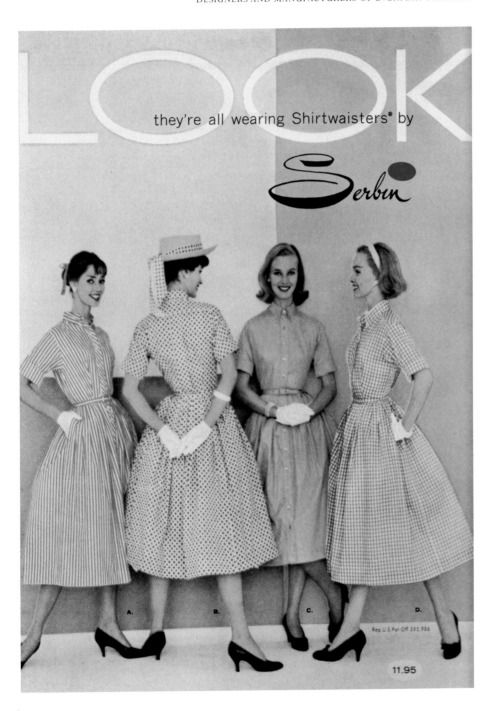

Tina Leser began making sportswear and daywear in Hawaii. In 1953, she formed her own company, Tina Leser Originals, in New York. Leser perfected toreador slacks with hostess tunics or sweaters. She was also known for swimsuits with coordinating cover-ups.

Tom Brigance had been a designer at Lord & Taylor until he created his own company in 1949. He received a Coty award in 1953 and became known for the sportswear he designed for various firms during the 1950s.

Vera Maxwell designed under her own New York-based "Vera Maxwell Originals" label from 1947 until 1964. She won a Coty Award in 1951 and Neiman Marcus Award in 1955.

Advertisement for Tina Leser, from *Vogue* magazine, August 15, 1955.

TOPS AND BOTTOMS—
AMERICAN HATS AND
SHOES

W ITH THE EXCEPTION of cocktail parties, where hats were treated as glamorous accessories, going hatless was on the rise during the 1950s. However, some enticing styles throughout the decade caused women to venture back into the millinery salon. In the early 1950s, shell-shaped caps were the most popular style, except during summer when wide-brimmed hats were preferred. Worn straight on the head, the hat styles looked their best with hair pulled into a chignon at the back of the head. Keeping in step with the tweedy, textured woolens of fashion, fuzzy materials like beaver fur felt were first used for millinery in 1952.

In 1954 deep "Juliette" caps and berets looked fetching when worn with hoop earrings and the chic short Italian "gamine" haircut popularized by Audrey Hepburn in the film *Sabrina*. Shoulder-length bobs also gained popularity, often worn off the face with the aid of a headband.

A flourish of hats blossomed in 1956 as part of the Edwardian revival created by the Broadway play *My Fair Lady*. A big, important-looking hat became an essential part of the look in 1956—an exotic silk turban or a garden of flowers growing on the brim of a wide-brimmed straw hat for spring was replaced by an even larger toque or fur beret, or feathered wide-brim style for fall and winter. The French twist became the leading coiffure for its ability to support these bulkier hats.

By 1958, hair was becoming more coiffed. Women added poufs and bangs and curls to their evening hairstyles, simple pageboys and shoulder-length bobs were passé, and a ponytail was not seen on any girl over the age of ten. For day, the hair became more bouffant, in bouncy, airy styles, brushed full at the sides, and often with bangs. When hats were worn, they tended to be simpler, draped satin toques or feathered helmets that imitated bouffant hair. For winter, a fur hat of leopard, mink, or otter was popular.

Hats dramatically dropped in use in 1959, as they crushed the bouffant hairdo consisting of petals of hair curving around the head or tossed like a salad of leaves. When hats were worn, they were tall, often brimless, like an upside down flowerpot. In strong colored felts, these hats paired well with

See-through vinyl was a popular material for making shoes, in whole or in part, after the 1950 Disney movie *Cinderella* debuted. However, although the clear vinyl may have imitated the look of a glass slipper, the material did not breathe. Black suede pump with clear vinyl vamp, c. 1952–54.

tweed suits and shapeless, brushed wool coats, reviving a 1920s look. When the hats were exploding with ice cream-colored flowers, they were perfect for wedding parties and summer events.

At the opposite end of the silhouette, black suede pumps with round-toes and midheight heels were the biggest volume-selling style early in the decade. Introduced from Italy in 1950, the "barely there" sandal that consisted of little more than a sole with some tiny straps became popular for dressy late-day and evening wear. The sandal became even barer when a revolutionary toeless and backless shoe was introduced from the Italian workshop of Ferragamo in late 1951. Called the "'band'" shoe, the style consisted of a single strap across the instep. The style was a hit in the summer of 1952, but there was a problem: the single strap meant the shoe had a tendency to slide off too easily. The problem was solved in 1954 when Beth Levine, wife and chief designer for her husband's New York company Herbert Levine, improved upon an existing patent for an orthopedic elastic insole. Levine's adaptation of the patent, which she called a "magnet-sock," made it possible for women to even run in a pair of single-strap shoes. The original patent holder quickly reestablished his claim and renamed the style "Spring-o-lator."

Footwear became more vibrant by 1955 as colorful shoes became popular. Satin pumps or sandals were dyed to match evening gowns, and daytime bags often were made to coordinate with shoes.

Shoe technology changed when an aluminum pin or shaft was first used as the core of a plastic heel, allowing their shapes to become impossibly thin.

Several European designers take credit for creating and naming the heel "stiletto," after a short-bladed knife, in 1954, but in the United States it was Delman who first presented the new skinny heel to Americans in 1956. The following year, a sharp, pointed toe was combined with the stiletto, and within a season, the extremely pointed toe and stiletto heel style dominated shoe fashions for the rest of the decade and into the 1960s.

Bernardos was founded by Bernard Rudofsky, a designer and historian. His wife Berta made samples based on his research of ancient Roman sandals and went into the commercial production of sandals in 1947. They were one of the first American shoe companies to have their footwear made in Italy.

Brown Shoe Company was celebrating its diamond jubilee in 1953. Over the years, the St. Louis shoe company had acquired many smaller companies and launched many brands, including Naturalizer (since 1927), Connie (since 1931), and LifeStride (since 1940). Newer lines included Jacqueline, Risque, Air Step, and Westport.

Capezio began as a theatrical shoe manufacturer in New York but went into fashion footwear in the 1940s when ballerina slip-on shoes were first shown in fashion shoots. Ben Sommers, the designer during the 1950s, received a Coty award in 1952 and a Neiman Marcus award in 1953.

David Evins became the first designer to be credited on any shoe manufacturer's label when he designed for I. Miller. He also designed shoes for Mainbocher, Charles James, and Norell, and counted First Ladies and film stars as his clients.

Dunn & McCarthy were located in Auburn, New York, and were known for their comfort-fitting shoe brands Enna Jetticks and Hill and Dale.

Embroidered and rhinestone-studded silk brocade shoes with custom-painted soles, by David Evins, c. 1957.

Blue shantung
pumps with black
diamente trim on
heels, c. 1958–60,
by Delman, a high-
end shoe line
created by Herman
Delman in 1919,
and sold to
General Shoe
in 1954.

Emme hats was a New York millinery founded by three women. In the 1950s, their designer was Adolfo Sardinas, who received a Coty award in 1955 and Neiman Marcus award in 1959 for his hat designs.

General Shoe began as a shoe chain before going public and acquiring other companies, including the Carlisle Shoe Company in 1954 and Herman Delman in 1955. Their top brands in the 1950s included Mademoiselle (created in 1954), Mannequin, Valentine, and Fortunet. General Shoe diversified into apparel and renamed themselves Genesco in 1959.

Herbert Levine and Beth Levine founded their New York shoe company in 1948. Herbert managed the business while Beth headed design. The Levine team received a Neiman Marcus award in 1954, largely for their work in creating the Spring-o-lator, as mentioned above.

International Shoe Co. was created by the amalgamation of several St. Louis firms and later acquisitions, including Florsheim in 1953. Their most popular brands in the 1950s were Accent and Vitality.

Johansen had been founded in St. Louis but moved to Corning, Arkansas, in the late 1940s to save on labor costs. The company was known for producing quality, affordable footwear under the Johansen label.

John-Frederics was a New York millinery founded by John Harberger and Frederic Hirst. In 1948, John Harberger left to start Mr. John hats, and Frederic Hirst retained the John-Frederics label.

Johnson, Stephens and Shinkle Shoe Co. were a St. Louis shoe company and produced the popular brands Matrix and Rhythm Step during the 1950s.

Gold fabric "Spring-o-lator" mule studded with aurora borealis rhinestones, c. 1958, by Herbert Levine.

Julianelli shoes were the product of Charles and Mabel Julianelli. Charles was in charge of production, and Mabel headed design of their New York business. Mabel was known for her dressy sandals and received a Coty award in 1950.

Mr. John was a New York millinery founded in 1948 by John Harberger. John P. John, as he was also known, had founded John-Frederics with Frederic Hirst in 1929, but, as noted earlier, Hirst retained the John-Frederics label when the partnership was dissolved.

Newton Elkin designed from his hometown in Philadelphia, working under the Pandora brand of shoes as well as a line under his own name.

Nusrala Shoe Company was a St. Louis shoe manufacturer known for the popular brands Da Venci and La Pattie.

Palizzio was founded by brothers Reuben and Leo Gordon in New York in 1950. Their head designer until 1954 was Florence Otway.

Qualicraft was the affordably priced store brand made for the Bakers-Leeds shoe chain in the United States in the 1950s and afterward.

Queen Quality was a top-selling brand of shoes originally produced at the Thomas Plant factory in Jamaica Plains, Massachusetts. When the factory was sold in 1941, the new owners renamed the company after the brand.

Seymour Troy produced custom shoes under his own name, as well as a ready made collection under the name "Troylings." He was given the first Mercury Award of the National Shoe Industry Association in 1960 in recognition of thirty-five years of pioneering design.

United States Rubber Company was the first to offer women's tennis shoes in a variety of colors under the brand Kedettes, a division of their successful Keds line, which had been around since 1916.

United States Shoe Corporation was originally created from the amalgamation of eight Cincinnati shoe manufacturers to which Joyce shoes was added in 1955, followed by Selby in 1957. Their best-selling brands were Red Cross shoes, Cobbies, and Socialites.

Wolff Shoe Co. began when Samuel Wolff bought a shoe factory that had just gone out of business in Washington, Missouri, in 1949. Wolff produced women's fashion footwear under the brand name "Deb Shoes" beginning in 1950.

Advertisement for Kedettes, colored cotton sneakers by the United States Rubber Company, from *Vogue* magazine, March 1, 1959.

FURTHER READING

Hall, Marian. *California Fashion*. Abrams, 200▓

Milbank, Carolyn. *New York Fashion*. Abrams,

McDowell, Colin. *McDowell's Directory of Twen*
Prentice-Hall, 1985.

New York Times online archive: www.NYTim▓

Vogue magazine

Harper's Bazaar magazine

Seventeen magazine

LIFE magazine

So practical for summer

These SWIRLS meet every aspect of
your summer world. They plunge
low and lovely...whisk on with
carefree grace...open flat for
easy ironing. Sanforized cottons.
The paint-splash print on black,
brown or green, 10 to 18, about $8.
The pin-point broadcloth
check, in brown, blue or gray,
10 to 20, about $6.

Advertisement
for Swirl, from
Vogue magazine,
May 1, 1950.

INDEX